The EGG

Shelley Gill

Illustrated by
Jo-Ellen Bosson

iai Charlesbridge

For my little egg
Kye,
who cracks me up
and
for my mom—
thanks for hatching me
—S. G.

For my husband, Edward, who has helped me to realize my dreams and ambitions.
Thank you for your patience, encouragement, and sense of humor.
—J. C. B.

Text copyright © 2001 by Shelley Gill
Illustrations copyright © 2001 by Jo-Ellen Bosson

Published by Charlesbridge Publishing
85 Main Street, Watertown, MA 02472
(617) 926-0329 • www.charlesbridge.com

Printed in the United States of America
(hc) 10 9 8 7 6 5 4 3 2 1
(sc) 10 9 8 7 6 5 4 3 2 1

Illustrations done in gouache on Strathmore Illustration board
Display type and text type set in Caxton
Color separations made by Eastern Rainbow, Derry, New Hampshire
Printed and bound by Phoenix Color, Rockaway, New Jersey
Production supervision by Brian G. Walker
Designed by Diane M. Earley

SwC
J
591.468
Gill

16.95

Library of Congress Cataloging-in-Publication Data
Gill, Shelley.
   The egg / by Shelley Gill, illustrated by
Jo-Ellen Bosson.
      p. cm.
Summary: Describes how fish, birds, insects, and
other creatures lay eggs to reproduce and tells about
some stories and customs involving eggs.
   ISBN 1-57091-377-3 (reinforced for library use)
   ISBN 1-57091-378-1 (softcover)
   1. Embryology—Juvenile literature. 2. Eggs—
Juvenile literature. [1. Eggs.] I. Jo-Ellen Bosson,
1941- ill. II. Title.
QL956.5.G55 1999
591.4'68—dc21   99-18760

In the beginning the universe was silent.
Then came the cackle of a heavenly goose and
kerplopp . . . the "world egg" landed on a mound of mud.
   Sound goofy? Maybe to you. But this is one of the
many myths that mankind created to explain our
presence on the planet.

*Hindu people believed that a cosmic golden egg was split in two
by Brahma, who made the heavens from one half and the earth
and everything on it from the other.*

During ancient times, people from around the world believed the whole earth had once hatched from a single egg.

And why not? They had seen what looked like a rock begin to shake and crack, and out would climb a bird or snake or crocodile. Eggs are pretty amazing things!

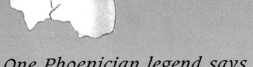

One Phoenician legend says God created heaven and earth from two halves of an egg.

In the South Pacific, the Samoans believed the heavenly one broke his egg home to pieces and flung them over the water. They became the Samoan Islands.

Scientists don't know exactly when the first eggs were laid, but eggs are a fairly new evolutionary invention. For about three billion years, when a living thing reproduced, it just split in two.

But nature doesn't put all its eggs in one basket. Eventually some animals began to lay eggs. Later, others began to keep their eggs inside their bodies.

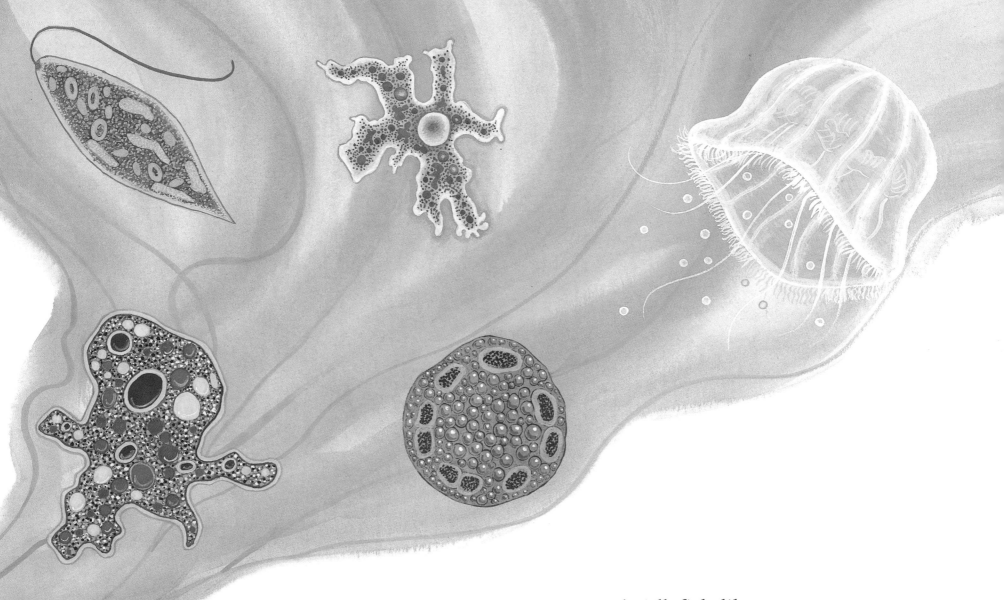

Simple jellyfish-like creatures
laid the first small, soft eggs,
in the oceans covering Earth.

Today most fish still lay their eggs, called roe, in the sea, or in rivers or lakes or streams. Some fish lay their eggs under a nest of air bubbles; other fish, like the Pacific salmon, dig a nest in gravel.

The dogfish—a kind of shark—lays eggs in an egg case called a mermaid's purse or skate barrow.

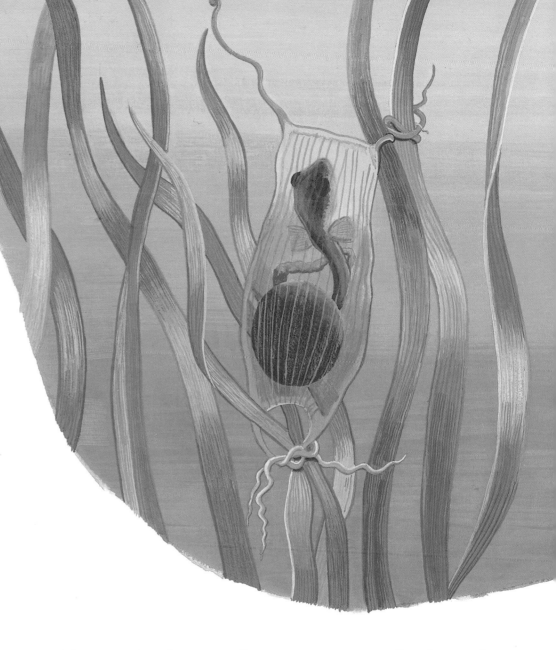

The grunion is sort of groovy. It's a surfer. It catches a wave and surfs onto the beach. The female lays her eggs, the male fertilizes them, and then they ride the backwash out again. Two weeks later a high tide pulls the fry—baby fish—out to sea.

Most sea creatures lay their eggs and leave, but not the octopus. A supermom, she lays 150,000 eggs, twisting them together in long ropy strands. Then she hangs them, loop after loop, from the roof of her cave. She keeps them clean by waving her tentacles through them and blowing streams of water on them.

A pregnant boy?! The female seahorse lays between two hundred and six hundred eggs through a tube into a pouch in the male seahorse's belly. As the baby horses grow, Dad's belly eggspands!

The animal that lays the most eggs is the American oyster. Laying one hundred million eggs at a time must be eggscruciating!

Long after the early sea creatures evolved, amphibians—creatures that live part of their life in water—developed. Then land reptiles and dinosaurs began to appear. Scientists think that instead of laying and leaving, some dinosaurs protected their eggs. Maiasaura was a particularly good egg. She built a mounded nest for her eggs and protected her babies after they were born. Her name means "good mother lizard."

One reptile, the American alligator, buries her eggs in a mound of vegetation. When they hatch, the babies emit high-pitched grunts. Mother gator comes running and digs them out with her forefeet and snout.

Gecko lizards lay a clutch of two eggs at a time, while python snakes lay as many as one hundred.

Atlantic green sea turtle hatchling

Can you remember being born? Some sea turtles might! When they are twenty to fifty years old, they return to their beach birthplace to lay their own eggs!

Atlantic green sea turtle

1 day

3-4 days

6 days

8 days

4 weeks

6-9 weeks

9 weeks

adult frog
16 weeks

12-16 weeks

9-12 weeks

Frogs and toads usually lay their eggs in water. They hatch as tadpoles, then grow legs and lungs to replace their tail and gills. Frogs lay eggs in a round clump. Toads lay theirs in strings up to fifteen feet long.

The Surinam toad of South America carries her eggs in little pouches on her back. The whole bunch hatch as toads and hop away, without ever swimming around as tadpoles.

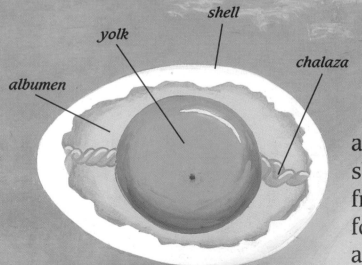

albumen yolk shell chalaza

As different animals evolved, many moved onto land, and a new kind of egg with a hard shell developed. The shell held moisture inside, so the egg could be laid away from water without drying out. There was also enough food stored inside the egg so that the embryo could grow and hatch completely formed. This was a big breakthrough!

The female emperor penguin lays its egg, then pushes it onto the male's feet. There the egg stays, protected from the ice and freezing Antarctic temperatures until the egg hatches, about eight weeks later. (Hmmmm . . . is it better to have egg on your face or eggs on your feet?)

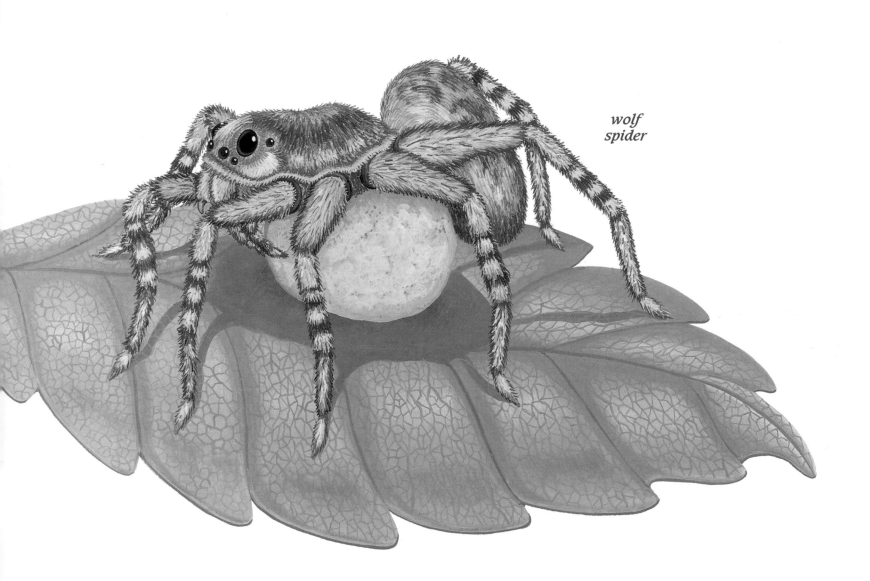

wolf spider

Spiders are eggstremely careful with their eggs. Some cover them with mud. Others wrap them in silk bags and carry them under their bellies.

Imagine the poisonous tarantula hawk wasp, who paralyzes her hairy spider prey, stuffs the living tarantula down a hole, and lays her eggs on top of it, so her babies will have a fresh snack handy when they hatch!

Bird eggs can be as small as a pearl or as big as a softball; round or shaped like a pear; white, speckled, or green, like the egg of the emu.

emu

sharp-shinned hawk

golden eagle

catbird

flicker

purple grackle

gallinule

red-winged blackbird

kingbird

murre

little gull

Many cliff-nesting birds lay pointed eggs that roll in circles, instead of rolling off cliffs.

Several species of birds, turtles, and crocodiles have an egg-tooth—a special tooth used by the young to break their way out of the shell.

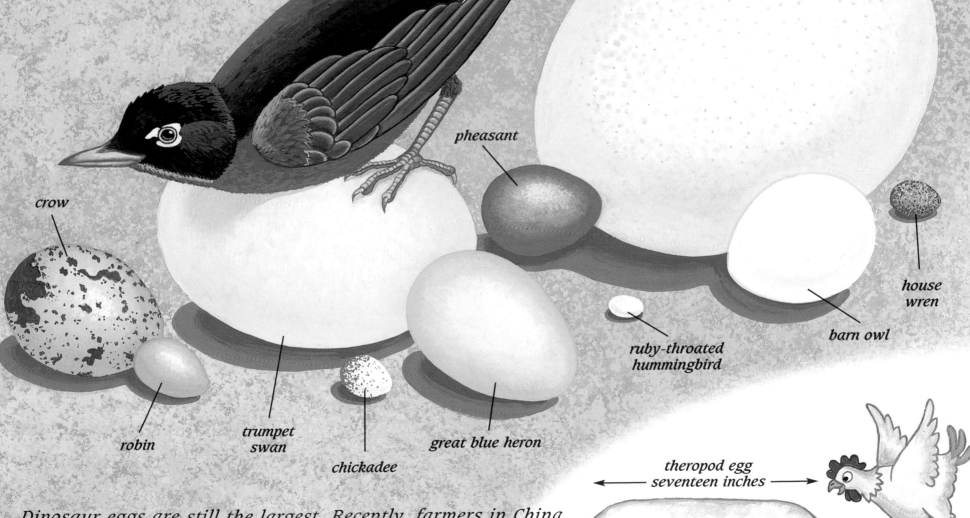

ostrich

pheasant

crow

house wren

barn owl

ruby-throated hummingbird

robin

trumpet swan

chickadee

great blue heron

theropod egg
seventeen inches

Dinosaur eggs are still the largest. Recently, farmers in China unearthed a pair of seventeen-inch-long elongated theropod eggs.

Many birds build nests for their eggs. Some birds collect grass or leaves, but others use special materials. Robins use a lot of mud and sticks, and flycatchers choose moss, lichen, and bark bound together by cobwebs. They may also include old snake skins!

robin

*female
ruby-throated
hummingbird*

*The eggsquisite hummingbird's nest may be made
from spider webs, moss, and dandelion down.*

The cuckoo bird—a rotten egg if ever there was one—takes an egg from a neighboring songbird's nest and replaces it with an egg of her own. Then she eats the stolen egg as a reward for her trickery! Once her egg hatches, the baby cuckoo soon outgrows the other baby birds.

young cuckoo chick

sedge warbler

The earth's first mammals may have laid eggs too, but as the mammals evolved, they protected their young by carrying the eggs inside their bodies, safe from predators and harsh weather. After the mother grows the egg inside her body, the father fertilizes it. The egg then develops inside the mother into a tiny mammal that looks like its parents when it is born.

Even you were once an egg!

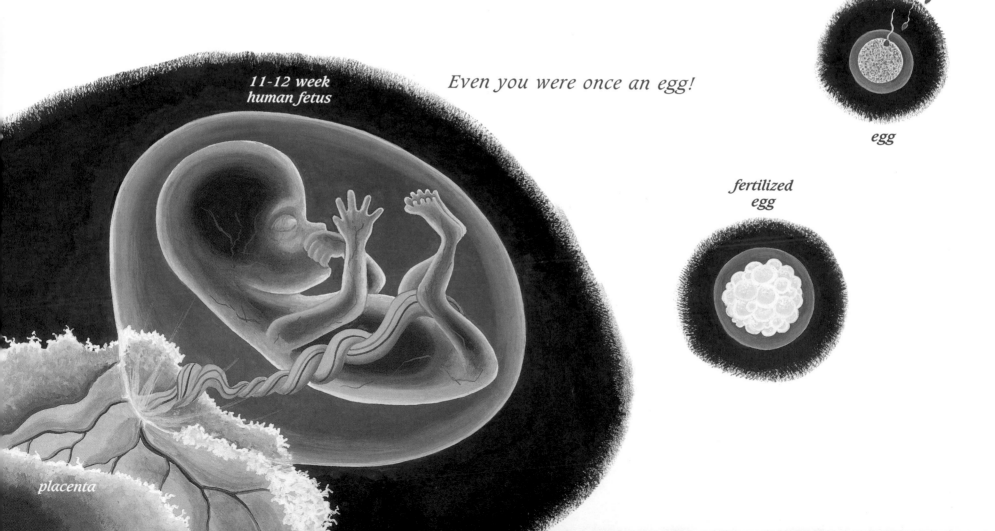

sperm

egg

11-12 week human fetus

fertilized egg

placenta

Can you name a mammal that still lays eggs? There are only three. The short-nosed echidna, the long-nosed echidna, and the duck-billed platypus lay eggs and have other things in common with reptiles.

short-nosed echidna

platypus

Human mothers carry their young inside their womb for nine months, then—yippee! When a baby is born it is time to celebrate! Pictures, presents, and nervous parents welcome the newborn into the world.

Some mothers put their babies in a pouch. Can you name any?

We humans know the egg as more than something that we have in common with fish, birds, reptiles, amphibians, and insects. It is also a powerful symbol. For centuries people believed that eggs had magical powers. People used eggs to drive away demons, call spirits, and cure sickness.

Eggs have long been a sign of peace.
The Chinese celebrated spring thousands
of years ago by giving each other
eggs dyed red, the color
of happiness.

Dream of eggs and
you'll soon be rich.

In France, a bride stepped on an egg as she entered her new home.

The Romany people buried eggs along the banks of rivers to prevent floods.

In some parts of the United States, people are superstitious about eggs. Finding a soft-shelled egg in a nest brings bad luck—unless you immediately throw it over your house!

Since ancient times, the egg has represented hope and new life. Now modern science is putting a new spin on that idea.

Recently, scientists fertilized the egg of a rare, nearly extinct African wildcat and then grew the embryo for five days in an incubator. After that, they froze it for a week at minus 373 degrees and then transplanted it into the womb of a plain old house cat. A few weeks later a new wildcat kitten named "Jazz" was born.

Scientists hope to prove that the eggs of soon-to-be-extinct creatures might be kept frozen for hundreds of thousands of years to be thawed when a suitable surrogate mother is found.

The eggstraordinary egg—the beginning
of life—where myth and science meet!

For further reading on eggs:

Heller, Ruth. *Chickens Aren't the Only Ones*.
Penguin Putnam Books for Young Readers, 1999.

Selsam, Millicent E. *Egg to Chick*. HarperCollins
Children's Books, 1987.

Johnson, Sylvia A. *Inside an Egg*. Lerner
Publications Company, 1982.

Jenkins, P. Belz. *A Nest Full of Eggs*. HarperCollins
Children's Books, 1995.

Lambert, David. *The Ultimate Dinosaur Book*. DK
Publishing, 1993.

Did you know that there are no eggs in eggplant?

Some useful web sites:

National Geographic Society. "Dinosaur Eggs."
http://www.nationalgeographic.com/dinoeggs/index.html (1996).
See photos and information about dinosaur eggs. You can virtually "hatch" three different
dinosaur eggs and find out how the embryos would look.

Parks and Wildlife Service, Tasmania. "Wildlife of Tasmania."
http://www.parks.tas.gov.au/wildlife/mammals/platypus.html (1997).
Features photos, facts, and further reading about the platypus.

Provincial Museum of Alberta. "Provincial Museum of Alberta."
http://www.pma.edmonton.ab.ca/vexhibit/eggs/vexhome/egghome.htm (1998).
Enjoy an extensive collection of 300 egg images plus facts, trivia, and Q&A about eggs.

Author Unknown. "Moe and Audrey, the Bearded Dragons."
http://www.lizardboy.com (1999).
See how the bearded dragon lays eggs, and watch the dragons on the live dragon cam.